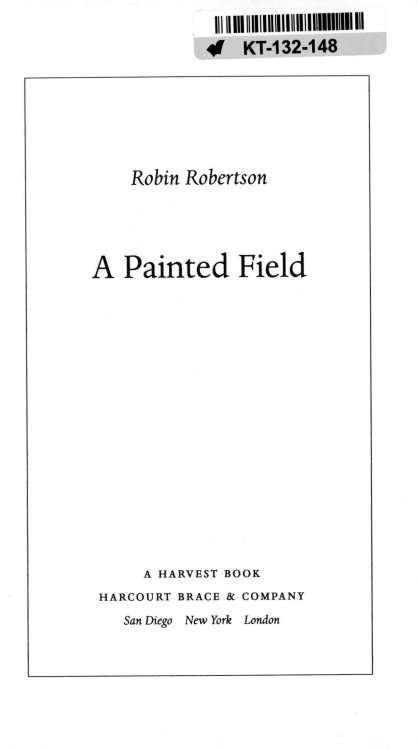

Robin Robertson

A Painted Field

A HARVEST BOOK

HARCOURT BRACE & COMPANY

San Diego   New York   London

KT-132-148

Copyright © Robin Robertson 1997

All rights reserved. No part of this publication may be reproduced
or transmitted in any form or by any means, electronic or mechanical,
including photocopy, recording, or any information storage and retrieval
system, without permission in writing from the publisher.

Requests for permission to make copies of any part of the work
should be mailed to: Permissions Department, Harcourt Brace & Company,
6277 Sea Harbor Drive, Orlando, Florida 32887-6777.

First published in Great Britain in 1997 by Picador,
an imprint of Macmillan Publishers Ltd.

Library of Congress Cataloging-in-Publication Data
Robertson, Robin
A painted field/Robin Robertson.—1st U.S. ed.
p. cm
ISBN 0-15-100366-1
ISBN 0-15-600647-2 (pbk.)
I. Title
PR6068.01925P35   1998
821'.914—dc21   97-27711

Text set in Dante
Designed by Lori McThomas Buley
Printed in the United States of America
First Harvest edition 1999
A C E F D B

A PAINTED FIELD

For Clare, Eilidh and Cait

CONTENTS

ACKNOWLEDGMENTS

Acknowledgments are due to the editors of the following:

After Ovid: New Metamorphoses (Faber), *Agni, Arvon Poetry Competition Anthology, Canadian Forum, College Green, Columbia, Cyphers, Descant, Forward Book of Poetry* (Faber), *Grand Street, Harvard Review, Independent, Irish Times, Listener, London Magazine, London Review of Books, National Poetry Competition Anthology, New Edinburgh Review, New Statesman, New Writing 5* and *6* (Vintage), *New Writing Scotland* (ASLS), *Observer, Pequod, PN Review, Poetry Review, Quarry, Rialto, Rilke in Engish* (Penguin), *Scotsman, Soho Square* (Bloomsbury), *Southern Review, Spectator, Stand, Sunday Times, Times Literary Supplement, Yale Review.*

'Artichoke,' 'At Dusk,' 'The Flowers of the Forest,' 'Hands of a Farmer in Co. Tyrone,' and 'Sheela-na-Gig,' were first published in *The New Yorker.*

'Camera Obscura' was published separately, in a limited edition, by Colophon Press. The poem was dramatised by BBC Radio Scotland and broadcast on Christmas Day 1997.

A number of these poems are included in *Penguin Modern Poets 13.*

The author was grateful for the opportunity to spend time in the Tyrone Guthrie Centre at Annaghmakerrig and at Hawthornden Castle.

A PAINTED FIELD

NEW GRAVITY

Treading through the half-light of ivy
and headstone, I see you in the distance
as I'm telling our daughter
about this place, this whole business:
a sister about to be born,
how a life's new gravity suspends in water.
Under the oak, the fallen leaves
are pieces of the tree's jigsaw;
by your father's grave you are pressing acorns
into the shadows to seed.

THREE WAYS OF LOOKING AT GOD

1.

A claustrophobia of sand and stone: a walled heat.
The light bleaches and curves like a blade, isolates
the chirr of crickets, seed-pods detonating,
the valley waiting in a film of flame.
A bird finds an open channel in the air
and follows it without exertion to the branch.

2.

The sky is slashed like a sail. Night folds
over the shears, the dye, the docked tails.
We listen to the rumours of the valley:
goats' voices, gear-changes, the stirring of dogs.
In the green light, lambs with rouged cheeks
skitter from their first communion, calling for home.

3.

Lightning flexes: a man chalked on a board, reeling,
exact, elementary, flawed; at each kick, birds flinch
and scatter from the white lawn.
The long trees bend to the grain of the gale,
streaming the dark valley like riverweed.
All night: thunder, torn leaves; a sheathing of wings.

ADVENT IN CO. FERMANAGH

Two chemists in one village,
side by side,
ours and theirs;
both specialise in cattle cures.
The greengrocer, meanwhile,
doubles as undertaker;
his potatoes
always hard and white,
beautifully laid out.

The town is bottle-shaped
and dressed for Christmas
in a Morse code of coloured lights,
marginal snow
in crescents at the windows,
and on the sill,
in the holly's gloss
of red and starred green,
illuminating angels.

Leaning men on corners watch
the circumspect, the continent,
linking their way to church.
Then the mid-day angelus
opens the doors in the street
like organ stops,
for the pinched and raddled
in their penitential suits
pulling children out of doorways:
strings of hankies from a sleeve.

No one watches the soldiers
walking backwards on patrol:
the cellophane crackle of radios,
the call and answer
as they stroll, each cradling
a weapon like a newborn child.

Stooped under hangovers,
the pasty supplicants
file towards the priest
to say 'Aaah' for atonement,
and shuffle out, cowed,
in a cold sweat,
His Body
tucked behind the teeth.

Doors disclose them,
scribbling down the hill
for rashers and egg
and wheaten bread;
Guinness and Black Bush:
gifts for the back room
with the curtains pulled.

Sunlight glints
like mica schist in granite
on the huddled homes
as the rain comes casting down.

Stone circles of sheep
in the drowned field
watch helicopters come
dreaming over hedges:

horse-flies the size of houses,
great machines
for opening the air,
and shaking it shut.
Leaving an absence, a silence,
and a hatch of light
which discovers a door.
The town drunk emerges
gingerly from the bar,
amazed by the familiar;
patting his pockets,
blinking like Lazarus.

STATIC

The storm shakes out its sheets
against the darkening window:
the glass flinches under thrown hail.
Unhinged, the television slips its hold,
streams into black and white
then silence, as the lines go down.
Her postcards stir on the shelf, tip over;
the lights of Calais trip out one by one.

He cannot tell her
how the geese scull back at twilight,
how the lighthouse walks its beam
across the trenches of the sea.
He cannot tell her how the open night
swings like a door without her,
how he is the lock
and she is the key.

SHEELA-NA-GIG

He has reached her island by stones
pegged in swollen water,
through rain that has fallen for days.

He touches the welling mouth, the split stone;
she shows him the opening folds
where rainwater troubles and turns.

The rain slows, and stops; light deepens
at the lid of the lake, the water creased
by the head of an otter, body of a bird.

THE FLAYING OF MARSYAS

after Ovid

I.
A bright clearing. Sun among the leaves,
sifting down to dapple the soft ground, and rest
a gilded bar against the muted flanks of trees.
In the flittering green light the glade
listens in and breathes.

A wooden pail; some pegs, a coil of wire;
a bundle of steel flensing knives.

Spreadeagled between two pines,
hooked at each hoof to the higher branches,
tied to the root by the hands, flagged
as his own white cross,
the satyr Marsyas hangs.

Three stand as honour guard:
two apprentices, one butcher.

II.
Let's have a look at you, then.
Bit scrawny for a satyr,
all skin and whipcord, is it?
Soon find out.
So, think you can turn up with your stag-bones
and outplay Lord Apollo?
This'll learn you. Fleece the fucker.
Sternum to groin.
Tickle does it? Fucking bastard,
coming down here with your dirty ways . . .
Armpit to wrist, both sides.

Chasing our women . . .
Fine cuts round hoof and hand and neck.
Can't even speak the language proper.
Transverse from umbilicus to iliac crest,
half-circling the waist.
Jesus. You fucking stink, you do.
Hock to groin, groin to hock.
That's your inside leg done:
no more rutting for you, cunt.

Now. One of you on each side.
Blade along the bone, find the tendon,
nick it and peel, nice and slow.
A bit of shirt-lifting, now, to purge him,
pull his wool over his eyes
and show him Lord Apollo's rapture;
pelt on one tree, him on another:
the inner man revealed.

III.
Red Marsyas. Marsyas *écorché,*
splayed, shucked of his skin
in a tug and rift of tissue;
his birthday suit sloughed
the way a sodden overcoat is eased
off the shoulders and dumped.
All memories of a carnal life
lifted like a bad tattoo,
live bark from the vascular tree:
raw Marsyas unsheathed.

Or dragged from his own wreckage,
dressed in red ropes
that plait and twine his trunk

and limbs into true definition,
he assumes the flexed pose of the hero:
the straps and buckles of ligament
glisten and tick on the sculpture
of Marsyas, muscle-man.
Mr Universe displays the map of his body:
the bulbs of high ground carved
by the curve of gully and canal,
the tributaries tight as ivy or the livid vine,
and everywhere, the purling flux of blood
in the land and the swirl of it flooding away.

Or this: the shambles of Marsyas.
The dark chest meat marbled with yellow fat,
his heart like an animal breathing
in its milky envelope,
the viscera a well-packed suitcase
of chitterlings, palpitating tripe.
A man dismantled, a tatterdemalion
torn to steak and rind,
a disappointing pentimento
or the toy that can't be re-assembled
by the boy Apollo, raptor, vivisector.
The sail of stretched skin thrills and snaps
in the same breeze that makes his nerves
fire, his bare lungs scream.
Stripped of himself and from his twin:
the stiffening scab and the sticky wound.

Marsyas the martyr, a god's fetish,
hangs from the tree like bad fruit.

STORM

Faulted silence, dislocation,
heat in the hissing trees;

June tightens to a drumhead
that the rain begins to beat:

pavane, charade, scheherazade.
The tattoo drills and drums

the masque through crystal;
frost and ice foreseen in sudden glass.

The rain-curtain rises to a hard silence
and the fresh world emptied like a drain.

TOKENS

Roofs folded in and stepped against
the sea's retaining wall:
where the gulls creak
in the knocking wind
and the sea is climbing the stones of the stair.

Stood
counting waves in the dark:
the seen pulse of a hidden drum.
Spinning out the six white stones to her,
the tokens.

Walking widdershins to a cold curve,
sea brink and stone collide: the coming night
become drenched rock, the churning wind;
waves become faces, their cries
becoming tide.

VISITING MY GRANDFATHER

In a room as dark as his
you remembered colour, in amongst
brown Bakelite, teak,
and felt for furnishing,
the black-out curtains from the war.
I saw the blue cuneiform of the crossword
looming under the magnifier
for my father to finish;
the slow valves of the radio
warming like coals
into English voices;
the rainbow spills, for his pipe,
in a beaker by the hearth.
And the fire, of course, when lit,
full of all the usual pictures:
caves, dragons, life.
But being children
we were out too far to feel the heat,
kicking our legs on the high chairs,
nursing our flat lemonade
and trying not to see our blurred ghosts
in the dresser's unsilvering glass.

Once a year, though, it was summer,
and in the great window
were the white yachts of Stonehaven,
the yellow yachts in the bay.
As if colour TV
had come to Scotland, all afternoon
we watched a testcard
of acid primaries

on wavelengths of green
and a lemony blue.

It was a chill parlour, despite the fire,
but leaving was like opening
the door of a fridge: cold
dumping on your sandalled feet,
your bare legs.
Finding my way back from the kitchen,
arms out in the dark
for the connecting door,
I came against
a womanly thing,
some kind of shawl
or handbag dressed in feathers,
which I felt all over,
putting my hands down below—
till I touched the wetness,
neck and sudden beak,
left it swinging as I ran,
leaving half my life behind
with the hung pheasant
and half in my hands with its blood:
cinnabar, carnelian,
rose madder, rust.

ABERDEEN

The grey sea turns in its sleep
disturbing seagulls from the green rock.

We watched the long collapse, the black drop
and frothing of the toppled wave; looked out
on the dark that goes to Norway.

We lay all night in an open boat, that rocked
by the harbour wall—listening to the tyres creak
at the stone quay, trying to keep time—
till the night-fishers came in their arc, their lap
of light: the fat slap of waves, the water's
sway, the water mullioned with light.

The sifting rain, italic rain; the smirr
that drifted down for days; the sleet.
Your hair full of hail, as if sewn there.
In the damp sheets we left each other sea-gifts,
watermarks: long lost now in all these years
of the rip-tide's swell and trawl.

All night the feeding storm banked up
the streets and houses. In the morning
the sky was yellow, the frost ringing.

The grey sea turns in its sleep
disturbing seagulls from the green rock.

PIBROCH

Foam in the sand-lap of the north-sea water
fizzles out—leaves the beach mouthing—
the flecks of the last kiss
kissed away by the next wave, rushing;
each shearing over its own sea-valve
as it turns with a shock into sound.

And how I long now for the pibroch,
pibroch long and slow, lamenting all this:
all this longing for the right wave,
for the special wave that toils
behind the pilot but can never find a home—
find my edge to crash against,
my darkness for its darknesses
my hands amongst its foam.

FIREWORKS

'In the greatness of the flame he gave up the ghost'
FOXE'S BOOK OF MARTYRS, XI

The poplars are emptied at dusk
like blown matches. A gust frees
and scatters the leaves in their last blaze:
the bronze husks catch and cartwheel
round and down the street to the park
in the smoke of a dark autumn,
from the thin, extinguished trees.

In the small lake, what had once been water
now was seamed with smoke,
marbled and macular,
dim and deep as wax,
with each stick and twig like a spilled wick
in the dulling hollow of the sconce:
metamorphosis in the cancelled pond.

By midnight the ice was dished, percussive,
blue-black under a bone moon.
Skipping stones on its steel deck
gave the sound of thrown springs,
railway lines, or fence-wire, singing.
I had scored a tracery of leaving, a map engraved,
a thrilling in the air.

After the park, the garden,
and the bright litter of the night's display:
a stubble of burnt-out cones and candles,
cold star-shells, burst and charred,
a catherine wheel fused to the bark;

scorched bottles, tapers; smoke, hanging;
the softening box on its bed of ash.

Hands cupped around a match's flame:
the blue twist of smoke. Petrol
is the fifth element: opening
a door in the night I can leave through.
Across the city, a scratch of light
disappears. I hear its stick
clattering in the trees.

A SHOW OF SIGNS

i.m. B.J.R. 1929–1990

Fleshed hibiscus, the first in five years,
opening: the way of blood in water.

In the loft a thrush lay folded.
A peacock steps behind the ilex trees.

Someone at night had sewn in
grief: a gathering shirr that drew us close, and closed.
Fear dragged and fluttered as a bird's wing would
when trapped, as we are trapped.

Death is first absence, then a presence
of the dead amongst the living:
the kick of grief like a turning fin, that whelms
but cannot break the surface.

Months from sight, our child begins to hear:
a muffled wash of sea beyond the wall.
What she will remember will be fear
—which sounds like shaken tin—
and the ache that swims beside her:
that she cries to, in mistake for hunger.

We have tasted salt;
we feel our eyes shine.

In the loft the thrush lies folded.
The peacock steps behind the ilex trees.

What we have known is life, broken;
what we have seen is a red flower open its face and die.

AFFAIR OF KITES

I sit, astonished by the pink kite:
its scoop and plunge, the briefness of it;
an escaped blouse, a pocket of silk
thumping like a heart
tight above the shimmering hill.
The sheer snap and plummet
sculpting the air's curve, the sky's chambers.
An affair with the wind's body;
a feeling for steps in the rising air, a love
sustained only by the high currents
and the hopeless gesture of the heart's hand.

The kitemaster has gone, invisible
over the hard horizon;
wind walks the grass between us.
I see the falling,
days later feel the crash.

BALE-FIRE

Each watcher wears a lighted mask
blazoned with the fire's gust,
like a birthmark cast from the kiln.
Heat in waves, in flames splashing,
and plumes, black plumes.

Sparks go up like spindrift,
crackling into the cold night flue.

The fire ebbs for the end of autumn:
cautery of ash and ember made
against the coming snow.
And the rain, immanent as stars,
now falling, falling slowly.

Under the shiver of a new moon: winter;
entering, charmed and charged.

IN MEMORIAM DAVID JONES

1.xi.1895–28.x.1974

The first day of winter
and the sun's long shadows
cover the leaves on the river path to the sea.
Fleeing moorhens drill across the water,
homeless now for the year's cold quarter;
it was a wild night put their reeds among these trees.

The river's speed prevents its freezing:
the hard thread of the undertow gives one more twist
and coasts out to the bay.
The path follows at a distance, rising
as the land is pulled up short, forced into cliff.
In this, as in all things, the ocean has its way.

The sun's slow burn is glazing the sky,
turning birds on its rim into glass.
From this high rock the sea is signal:
shaking saucers of light on water
lap like lanterns, shatter
into white-caps, into lifting gulls

that tilt at the sun and drop from its height,
laughing like indulgent fathers
down to the chopping sea;
they go fluent over wave and spray:
sleights of wing, beautiful deceits for each corrugation,
each new world in their way.

Cloud darkens the sea like gathering shoal
and a grey seal surfaces, astonished,
on a scene that stays the same;
sinks back phantom and is towed under—
has never tired,
will never tire of this.

AT DUSK

Walking through the woods
I saw these things:
a cat, lying, looking at me;
a red hut I could not enter;
the white grin of the snared fox;
the spider in a milk bottle,
cradling the swaddled fly,
rocking it to sleep;
a set of car keys, hanging from a tree;
a fire, still warm, and a bone
the length of my arm, my name
carved on it, mis-spelt.
The dog left me there,
and I went on myself.

FIRST WINTER

Come and see this, I called,
this red bird at the feeder,
this striate sky,
these things I've done.

By the time you look you've missed it,
these lines are cold, the sky mussed,
the snow-shy cardinal
newly gone.

LITHIUM

After the arc of ECT
and the blunt concussion of pills,
they gave him lithium to cling to—
the psychiatrist's stone.
A metal that floats on water,
must be kept in kerosene,
can be drawn into wire.
(He who had jumped in the harbour,
burnt his hair off,
been caught hanging from the light.)
He'd heard it was once used
to make hydrogen bombs,
but now was a coolant for nuclear reactors,
so he broke out of hospital barefoot
and walked ten miles to meet me in the snow.

RETREAT

In the abandoned house
the chairs are tipped,
the coffee cups thick with spoor;
rolled mattresses shift and sound
as the springs return
to the shape of the sleeper.
I have carried the cold in from outside
so find sticks for the grate
and throw in my diaries,
one by one,
'86 to '74.
The years burn well, the wood roaring;
the fire turns the pages,
reads each book backwards.

Outside, the trees stand like smoke;
the moon declines
behind a scarf of cloud.
I want to go where I am not known,
where there are no signs,
where the snow squeaks like polystyrene
on a discontinued path to the dark
knot of the forest.
I want to go somewhere
to let out this life like warm water
and lie there
clean and cold:
the steady heart's diminuendo,
a bag of pipes' diminishing drone.

ESCAPOLOGY

A shallow cut lets the blood bead:
and you could charm red bracelets,
coax necklaces from nowhere.
You stashed blades like savings,
pulled them out with a flourish
in a fan of silver.

Soon it was ribbons from the wrist
and sawing yourself in two; always
trying to disappear.
Then the finale: sedatives, restraints,
the escape-proof box. And you
lying there. A locked knife.

AFTER THE OVERDOSE

What surprised me most?
Coming home to an open door,
rose petals everywhere, the bed
incongruous with blood?
The paramedic's satchel
left behind in all the rush?

Or you in the hospital,
the crusted corners of your mouth,
the gown they'd put you in?
You never wore short sleeves,
not since you burned a name
into your arm with cigarettes.

Or, finally, that you weren't dead?
That surprised me. That regret.

FUGUE FOR PHANTOMS

This is the heart's thorn: the red rinse of memory;
this is the call of the coronach—keening, keening
over the water, haunted water,
the pitched grey, gull-swept sea.

This is the net and trident, thrown and retrieved,
thrown again; this is the death we live through—
our own thoughts are the mesh that's cast,
that let in the past with a stabbing spear.

These are the strange stigmata, the memories that
    bleed;
these are the luminous ghosts: lures
on the barb that pulls the heart from darkness
and silence, to the surface of the sea.

Where they have risen, the sea-dead, bobbing in effigy:
skin gone to curd, and worn now like a fragile dress,
water behind the eyes like the insides of oyster shells;
their huge heads puckered, their faces pursed like lips.

I would commit it all to the deep;
I want never to remember anything of this.

LUDIC

She felt like liver
in the spilling dark
and I was hard as an arm,

lopped at the wrist,
raw and rich still
with the lucid milt.

We gape and we are healed:
her mouth on me
like wind on an open wound.

NAVIGATING NORTH

He'd hitched out of Frankfurt
till the fog and the dark
turned the road to a loud ocean,
its headlights ropes of pearl.
He got out here—four hundred kilometres
from the sea—reminded of Aberdeen.

Three hours ago he'd been
fucking the chambermaid:
making her show the white of her teeth.
Then she fucked him;
the schnapps in the shot glass
shivering by the bed.

The adult channel had the room
flickering as she finished him off.
Swallowing his pride, he might have
glossed ten years ago,
tossing back his drink,
crashing it at the wall.

But here was a car graveyard in a pool
of sodium and glass. He'd cut himself
opening up the Audi he sat in now,
watching the lit sea
rock the light,
the night-fishers spilling their nets.

Stars fall from his hands,
his cut hands full of splinters
and herring-scales; his shirt slaked red.
He is navigating north
in a beached car; his hands shake
constellations on the floor.

BLOWING OUT THE LIGHT

After fourteen gins, the end
of this night's slipway
is an unmarked door, and this:
postcards and photographs tipped in
to the mirror's frame,
a few choice icons propped amongst ash,
cosmetics, spent matches;
the teddy bear is there
as if to cancel out the blister-pack of pills.
A poster of Paris, Doisneau's lovers;
a candle on the window sill.
Closing my eyes
I stitch the sheet with seed,
subside, and head for home.

SHOT

You sleep as I stumble
room to room, unhelmed,
heavy-greaved;
coming to you
through gorse-light
and the fallen trees:
heraldic, blessed
with wounds.
Red-handed at the key
I was stock-still, gazing back
at deer-slots in the snow:
flushed, quick from the kill,
carrying my shot,
my sadness like a stone.
In the quarry-hole of your bed
you're sleeping still.

HILL-FORT

'What we cannot hold we destroy'
ROBERT BRUCE, 1320

Enter the torc of trench and rampart,
stand on the beaten sill of earth
that rings round the spired hill.
Under a lintel of low sun, thinning branches,
step down, enter the spiral.

Broken by lightning, snapped in storm,
half of a great tree rests its perfect perpendicular
grey in the arms of a green neighbour; they stand there
deliberate as dolmens.
Walk through their door.

A sudden unhinging of air—
the gust throws up old leaves like scaring birds:
the birds wheel like ash,
the leaves tick down in a turning circle.

Here, the remains of a need-fire—
black tins, twists of paper,
smoke-spoor on the faces of trees.
The wind plays ash round the head of a cracked doll:
tilts the latch of the lids,
opens the eyes.

Pass on, past the fire, out of the ditch
and into the centre, pass on up to the oak.

Wind darkens the grass again,
tugs at the dead trees sleeved in ivy:
the low branches becoming whips
the high branches hands.
Autumn mines the land to detonate
the stray step, the patter of birds;
each twig a trigger
that will send a pheasant drilling up
through air that smells of rust,
a metal coil unwinding in the throat.

The pollard oak is smeared with creosote,
its cropped head on fire with mistletoe like smoke;
a red seal for every limb removed
and for every scar a new spike in the crown.
Wounds drive the roots deeper,
out like spokes to the hill's rim.
What we cannot hold we destroy, or attempt to
    destroy.
But the horned god carries cautery like a flag.

The wind finds a flute in the head of a wren.
The year is swinging shut.

JACK-IN-THE-GREEN

Grinning soldiers
patrolling the border with biscuits,

tricked out in a motley of green and grey,
sooty faces, and leaves
where their hair should have been.

We came across one in the garden,
crouching: the Green Man abroad,
a compost of flesh and grass and metal,

haunched like a dog caught
shivering at its stool.

HANDS OF A FARMER IN CO. TYRONE

He wore fish-gutter's gloves to pick brambles:
scoured leather, without fingertips,
so his fist could find the insides of the bush
and open around the soft black heart,
for the easing of the fruit.
He was a thorn in the fenced garden:
his hand at the command wire
paying out the line from culvert to sheugh.
They were on his land,
so he pulled the road up by the root.

FEEDING THE FIRE

Some hard, half-eaten logs
lie drifting in ash:
black in the flocculent
smother of grey.
Just a puttering flame,
the occasional spat of cinder.

Holding a sheet of the *Times*
up against it, though,
the lung of paper sucked in
and suddenly lit from behind:
a roaring diorama;
the long throats of fire, feasting,

hungry for news. The page is read,
then reddened, then consumed.

A DECOMPOSITION

The horse decoded on the killing floor:
a riddle of hair and bone
unknotted here
by a bad fall,
a buzzard, some
unkindness of ravens.
Then dogs came
for the dismantling:
splayed the legs to cord and cable,
emptied the chest,
snapped the brooches of the back.
The forelock sits
intact on the skull's white crown,
like a wig;
the head's cockpit
fizzing with maggots.
The horse drones.

Three days later,
a bone rebus;
the horse is parsed.
The ribs at sail, the body like a boat
in a surf of horsehair,
hollowed, resonant.
The wind's knife wedged in the keys
of an organ and left; the horse
playing itself, its singular note, its cipher.
A signature, legible and bold.

THE TRANSLATOR

He will go west
and west again,
striking out on his own
in open water.
Sewing the surface,
one quarter man
three quarters verb,
fitting his turbulence
to the undertow.

THE SPANISH DANCER

after Rilke

The audience in the cup of her hand,
she is a struck match: sparks,
darting tongues, and then the white flare
of phosphorus and the dance ignites
a charm of fire, uncoiling, spreading fast.

And suddenly she is all flame.

She is brazen: glancing round and shamelessly
setting her hair alight, turning her dress
to a seething inferno, from which she stretches
long white arms, and castanets, like rattlesnakes
woken, startled to their ratcheting and clack.

And just as quick, as if constricted
by the sheath of fire, she gathers it up
and casts it off in one high gesture,
and looks down: it lies there raging on the ground,
shed flame stubbornly alive.
Radiant, chin tilted in salute, she dispatches it
with a steely fusillade of feet:
stamps it, pounds it, stamps it out.

LAKELAND

Walking the marches of the sodden demesne
on the Great Northern Railway's
remaining rampart: the lost line
to Bundoran, closed these forty years.
This is not what they saw then, clutching
buckets and spades, rattling to the sea.

The causeway riding the fields
that steep in the water table;
tiers of orange piping, lashed concrete;
machines broken, submerged,
or given over to the clasp
of the wet, the slow assertions of nature.

A smashed cottage in a pool of slate,
the ground studded with stone bottles
of dandelion and burdock
drained in the dark; the pale
glans of mushrooms, a grasp of tubers,
sphagnum, horse-tongue, penicillin.

Nothing grows here but water.
The peat-cuttings are trenched
full of it: rows of the same sky
reflected line after line,
the peat in black shelves
like chests of drawers, drying out.

The heel-tugging clart thickens back to grass,
plastic fertiliser bags, broken glass.
Walking the embankment of an inland sea
reclaiming itself from the land; just making out
the line to Bundoran: the children dreaming
of sandcastles, under sun and a desiccant sky.

MOVING HOUSE

I. Middle Watch, Battersea

Wash of traffic: the crush
of waves on a windowed shore;

the windows, worn to a shiver, let in rain.
The wind is posting litter through the door.

Behind the gas-fire in the hearth
a soot-fall clears the chimney's throat

and the wind sings wire-songs: the filament
blown like coal to a white gasp.

A scuffle in the skirting-board
as something frees itself from something else.

The bulb stirs and the room shifts
twice towards the cellar door.

II. Defrosting

The satisfying creak and give
of another white slab: ridged,
tectonic, holding the ice-box shape
in a curved mould; as if the polystyrene
once packed around the fridge
now packed inside, heavier and cold.
Small ice clatters in the salad drawer
as I hack at the top with a knife,
hands raw and hot in the sharp snow.
Bored, I take a warm beer through and write.
The fridge ticks with water, dripping;
the kitchen bobs towards me in the night.

ARTICHOKE

The nubbed leaves
come away
in a tease of green, thinning
down to the membrane:
the quick, purpled,
beginnings of the male.

Then the slow hairs of the heart:
the choke that guards its trophy,
its vegetable goblet.
The meat of it lies, displayed,
up-ended, *al dente,*
the stub-root aching in its oil.

OYSTER

Bandage your hand
against the bladed shell,
work the knife well into the slot
(imagine a paint-scraper at a rusted rim)
and prise the lid off,
keeping the juices in.

Raise carefully to the chin
then bite the tongue out by the root:
suck it from its mouth of pearl
and chew, never swallow.
This is not sex, remember;
you are eating the sea.

BLIND MAN EATING WINKLES

Opening the door with a pin
he grubs for purchase,
tugging free
the firm twist of meat;
chewing it
as he roots out the next.

Specked with the rust-brown
circles, translucent as scabs,
he could sit here forever:
the rustle of the paper bag,
the shells scraping, the rummage
and shuck of the waves.

SILVER LAKE, VERMONT

Familiar gestures in a fresh hand:
the lint and balsam,
sanctuary of the cooled flesh.
Under a tissue moon, your hair untied,
your hair held back, the balm
of chrism dribbed against your side.

THE IMMORALIST

In the sleeping ward, night-nurses
gather at my curtained bed,
looming like Rembrandts, drawing
their winged heads in around
the surgeon at my side.
The golden section lit by anglepoise:
the wrinkled fruit, some books,
my chest strapped like a girl's
to stem the leaking wound.

Scissoring the grey crêpe
released a clot dark as liver:
an African plum in its syrup
slid into my lap.
Jesus, I said, as the doctor called for swabs,
more light, the stitching trolley.
Without anaesthetics he worked quickly,
his pale hands deft
as a guitarist at the frets.
This is what they'd been waiting for:
one hand at the pliant flesh,
the other subduing it with suture
and a blurred knot.
Five minutes and it was over,
and he was smiling at the Gide
amongst the magazines and grapes:
Used to be just TB, this place, he said,
my blood on his cheek like a blush.

As the nurse drew back the curtain, she warned:
There will be pain.
Night flooded, streaming slowly into shape;
I heard the tinnitus of radio,
saw the humped figure under his lung of light,
the earphones' plastic stirrup on its hook,
his left hand in place on the white bandage
his right hand holding my book.

CAMERA OBSCURA

for my father

Unto the Upright There Ariseth
Light in the Darkness
PSALM 112, V.4

Through the open door, and the latticed window,
light enters the dark room.

—⟋⟍—

*This morning I watched the sun take fire in the tops of the
lime trees that edge and fill the dark valley below me: the
Water of Leith. From our new house I looked out for my
new wife, walking in the Pleasure Grounds that terrace
down to the river's bed. She was wearing today the damask
dress I bought her on the joyous news that we will have a
child.*

*It was to my alarm that I spied suddenly a flash of red
on the far side of the ravine, high over the water. After a
few fretful moments I saw clearly that it was but a red
sheet being laid out by a maid to dry. Closing my eyes I
was troubled by the fetch of green the image left against a
white ground. It vexes me still.*

19 Moray Place, May 1838

—⟋⟍—

*Our first-born, Charlotte, four months old today. Ann is
stronger.*

*I do no painting now: some sketches only, studies; all
too dark, and not Academy style.*

*When a child is brought forth, the woman knows she must
carry on, I believe. The man knows he can die.*

May 1839

59

—⚬—

THE FLOWERS OF THE FOREST

Shouldering my daughter
like a set of pipes
I walk her
to a dead march
and counterpoint her crying
with my hummed drone:
the floo'ers o' the forest
are a' wi'ed awae

my cracked reed
blanking
on the high note,
the way a nib runs dry
in the rut it makes,
and splays.

—⚬—

'My young love said to me, "My mother won't mind,
And my father won't slight you for your lack of kind."
Then she turned her head to me, and this she did say,
"It will not be long, love, till our wedding day." '

—⚬—

CIRCUS ON CALTON HILL

Edinburgh burns below us,
this blazing day
where flame's invisible, a dark wave
lapping at the petrol's grain, as the fire-eaters
assuage their thirst.
The fanned embers of the city rustle
like the wrappers of sweets; heat
tinkering in the coal.
Sitting under the colonnade,
we are so close we almost touch.

Tumblers flip and flex,
desultory on the dry grass;
gulls channer in the stunned heat,
shedding air above us
and over the baking Craigleith stone,
to bank away to the airish Firth
and Inchkeith Island,
the Ferry and the May.
I watch you watching jugglers; the obligatory
lovers, and a snake-woman swallowing a sword.

You are turning heliotropic in this
acropolis of light, barely breaking sweat.
Lifting your hands to your hair a drop
runnels down under one arm to its cup
and the swell of your breast, and I am brimming,
scalding, kittling in the heat,
aching for you at the root of my tongue.
But I cannot find you; as you focus on the girl,

the girl on the grass below: her eyes closing,
her soft mouth as she bends to his.

—◊—

Could I find your face, or mine,
in these mirrors? Could I bring you back
with this coherent light?

—◊—

FOUR VIEWS FROM THE CAMERA OBSCURA

A herringbone of pends and wynds,
tenements in a guddle on top of each other
with a common stair like a street on its end;
the stone cliffs of the city scarped
as steep as the trap rock;
the high *lands,* smoking hives.

In Princes Street Gardens
a grey man holds his daughter up to pee,
her dress up about her, and him shaking.
But he is not her father,
his trousers at his knees,
their Tennent's Lager spilling in the grass.

To the Old Waverley: through the giant Y and H
of its sign, through the net-curtain gap
to the room inside, a lobster-pot of macramé,
sweltry, gravid: the German video on
with the sound down: the threshing hotel bed,
abandoned drinks. The red mesh of scorpions.

You are in another country, I know, but I did
just see you on that corner, clearly,
then passing in that cab, head down,
dashing me a note perhaps. The sap of you
still on my hands. A trace.
Wait. Wait for me here.

—⚊—

28 INVERLEITH ROW

Staring out at the Arboretum,
I see one tree shudder, disengage,
and move out of frame,
resolving itself
into a spider.
I pull back from infinity
and find the glass fledged
with frost: a strung web
and a thin fish-bone
ferning every edge.

—⚊—

She put her hand on me,
the bud of her hand on mine,
and in my withering hands she died.

—⚊—

I am forty. These last years I have lost my second child,
who died too soon to name, a daughter; and now my wife,

Ann, whose heart was never strong & was by this grief quite broken. Her suffering over, thanks be to God.

I have put down my painting & become an illustrator. For this I am now known. An illustrator, aged forty.

May 1842

—⬥—

PRIMARY

Winged before she could walk.
An X-ray would have shown the shadow
on the liver: a blur of feathers.
She was held up at the high window
to wave to me, down on the bright grass below;
I cannot now recall her face, or any sound,
only the way her fingers fell
in a flurry, beating on the glass.

—⬥—

When I think of the womb of my daughter
—small as a thimble—I despair.

—⬥—

THE GIFT OF TANTALUS

After-images, the after-shocks of lives
lived here, still troubling the light.
As land consecrated by battle,
we return to places
where things happened

just to feel the air thrill,
know that what we came to find
is fading, leaching away,
while the place mocks us,
flashing up our mortality,
our young ghosts,
in a time-lapse film
of flowers and rotting fruit.
Dark replaces light, the trace
of happiness is grief.
We stand in our own spoor
listening for laughter,
hungry for a youth that's out of reach.

—⚌—

This lobster vanity draws me
to the mirror in the creel.

—⚌—

FOUR VIEWS FROM THE CAMERA OBSCURA

The lens loses you in a blaze of traffic,
the murk of wynds; I track to the mouth
of Riddle's Court, to Lady Stair's Close,
but it clouds and I cannot find you. A clutch
of backpackers blocks my view, then the sun opens
and you are there. Your hair, your hand. A touch.

Driven through the wood's deep gully
the milling sheep were white water:
a shouldering slalom in the trees.
The river purls, its working muscle

turning in the tight glen below;
foam on its sides like a fleece.

Dawn: the harbour's curve
of stone—the shirr
of wind-flaw on water,
the falling of birds,
a woman waving
once from a window.

Both hands to her hair,
to the back of her head and the nape
of the neck, adjusting or unloosening
the warm braid in its simple knot;
the hair damp and heavy in her hands,
the root of each arm laid open and bare.

—〰—

FLAGS OF AUTUMN

Thorn grows flat against the flank of Calton Hill,
wind grooming the close wall
has disinclined the snappers
in the tour-coach below; they stay inside.
The empty lanyards slap against the poles.

To the south, the castle, Arthur's Seat:
basalt wedges, door-stops
holding open history.
Skeins of the tour-guide's commentary
ravel past the rock
in snatches; the lone piper
tugs on a cigarette
and marches back to his car:

gonfalons of Gold Leaf
fray and separate behind.

To the north, the bright regalia
of the panel-beaten Firth.
A squall lifts the gorse
at the brink of the sea-fall:
the sky's film turned to fast-forward
as clouds bloom
like milk in water.
The rabbits scud and veer
through the flattening grass
and disappear with summer.

Put up like kites in the pulling rain, gulls
skirl their greeting over the stones.
And where we sat, stunned, that day,
those months ago: crows strut. Their black flags
flare and gutter in the gale.

—⚡︎—

Desire becomes sorrow
just as night follows day
and today becomes tomorrow.

—⚡︎—

*Today the temple was rent and Free Men broke the shackles
of Government & the Crown. Five hundred Clergy at this
great event resigned their homes & livings, intent to follow
the Moderator and their consciences in Right Dissent out
of St. Andrews and the Establishment, to walk in proud*

procession to a Free Church of Scotland. The Enlightenment has found its fulcrum here.

I shall paint this turbulent Spectacle. It will be the great work. My testament.

May 1843: The Disruption

—⁊⁊—

How will I begin to say what I have seen? Sir David Brewster (a true man of the Renaissance) has introduced me to Mr. Adamson: a young scientist of prodigious gifts. I believe there is a future for me here.

In his studios at Rock House, Calton Hill, he has demonstrated how I might get the likenesses of all the many hundred ministers before they are dispersed. It is a method called the Calotype: a form of printed light that renders Nature in all truthfulness. By its employment one might match the finished work, in charcoal, chalk or sepia, of any great Master. Furthermore, it will serve as an aid to the Engraver, and to makers of portraits & landscapes and tableaux vivants. But much more than this, it is—in itself—a kind of Art.

It is thus both an ending and a beginning. The very crux.

May 1843: A Union

—⁊⁊—

I am ever impressed by the steady industry of my excellent friend Mr. Adamson in the face of poor health—his im-

provements to the Calotype process come daily. We are truly engaged upon great & noble work. Out of physics and chemistry Talbot made his photogenic drawing. From a collaboration between Science & Painting we have created a new Art.

The clergy interest me less, now, than the fish-wives and the pilots of Newhaven—the boys of Merchiston and the graves of Greyfriars. The Disruption Picture I have put aside. Tho' I have not yet let my palette dry, these light-drawings are my principal endeavour: to my eyes they are themselves paintings, and are marked with a more singular Truth. As I tell Nasmyth, the oils must wait now on the silver and the salt.

May 1844

—⁓—

Here, in the heart of our nation's city, at the city's vertex, approaching the median of this remarkable age, here have I found my prime meridian. The light I have looked for all my life is here: the light that reveals the truth of our selves in all our singularity and imperfection. It has released my pent Soul, my latent image.

Sol fecit, as my amiable friend has it: impressed by the agency of light alone.

Compare all this to M. Daguerre's stiff icons, his relics under glass! That secret mirror of vanitas, or this true world with all its flaws, caught in the very fibres of paper just as paint on the canvas.

At Rock House, May 1845

—⚏—

The colour green is our great difficulty. It seems it will not be reproduced.

Last night I dreamed I found her next to me: raven hair and red dress, more beautiful than ever. I looked again and she was clothed in sea-green—now white-haired, and her face gone black.

May 1846

—⚏—

I will often gaze out on the city from our high garden here: the spires & domes, the Castle, the Pentlands beyond, before my eye returns to the view below: the cemetery and gaol— the inmates of both guarded by their own Panopticon. This my Soul loathes.

Rock House, May 1847

—⚏—

I cannot always hold your hand
or cover your eyes,
my beautiful blue-veined daughter.

—⚏—

SECURING SHADOWS

The photographic light eats the plate
to make the moment hold,

but the subject has grown older
while the print is being made,
and is older still
when the paper finally dries.
All eyes have cataracts
from the blur of blinking,
all faces, deathmasks, rising
from their twins like wraiths.
We have caught the *memento mori*,
the injuries of time, and coloured them
bruise-blue and sanguine. Lovers,
exposed by corpse-light.

—⁓—

My young friend is dead. Everything I was not—and more.
The authentic contriver and manipulator of all our art; a
gentle spirit of most praiseworthy perseverance. Taken
from life. Four and a half years is all the time we had. He
was twenty-seven. I am now forty-six, and closer now
to Heaven. I have abandoned all this. As it has aban-
doned me.

May 1848

—⁓—

DUMB SHOW, WITH CANDLES

Still as a battlefield, the strewn city
goes under, slips into silhouette.
Some threads of smoke,
the lift and fall of flags in orange light.
The glinting windows go out one by one.

Low over the Firth, a fork of geese
comes pulling past, straight-necked:
creaking like rowlocks
over the frozen hill.
On the Parthenon below, querulous gulls
screel and skraik and peel away,
bickering, into the air's tow.
Too cold, even for them.
I circle the observatory one more time:
mine the only footprints in the snow.

Now the night has fallen, Edinburgh comes alight
as if each building's shell
has a fire inside that burned. The follies
—lit exhibits—stand here on the hill
in their white stone; the Castle glows.
And the streets are bright blurs of sodium
and pearl: the drawn tracery of headlamps
smeared in long exposure. For miles west
the city stretches,
laid with vapour trails and ghosts.

To the east, the folding sea has drowned
the girning of the gulls. A lighthouse
perforates the night: a slow cigarette.
Then there is no more light,
and no more breath or sound.

—⁂—

'She stepped away from me and she moved through
    the fair,
And so fondly I watched her move here and move
    there,

Then she went her way homeward with one star
   awake,
As the swan in the evening moves over the lake.'

—∞—

POLARITY

I begin to wish for the simplicities of war:
unison, delirium, a trance of order
in half-light: good and bad
accorded each a uniform.
To survive or die,
not let the side down or turn tail;
not to be here in this mire
of sidelong glances, tired lies.
To have colours to fly and follow:
a god, or rod of empire, an honourable madness;
to be part of this, or some such simple life.

—∞—

*I have lived my life in the camera obscura, working the
mirrors and gazing avidly at the world outside, the gloom
lit by the living image. Depth without definition, sight with-
out sound. No contact or communication. Platonic shadows
slipping out of view. I have lived my life transfixed by a
bright disc in a dark room.*

May 1849

—∞—

FOUR VIEWS FROM THE CAMERA OBSCURA

In the Grassmarket, a girl in a red dress
steps between parked cars
into the forensic flash, flash of cameras.
Around her, the Pre-Raphaelite beauties
of Julia Margaret Cameron,
the mongols of Arbus.

Track east to the Calton
where Nelson's upturned telescope
stands staring at the ground,
where the observatory lies vacant, closed
a century ago by railway smoke
from Waverley: the Enlightenment below.

Gulls mill like ash around Valhalla,
over Calton Hill and the empty High School,
modelled on the Temple of Theseus,
the dark, echoing shell of independence.
The sooty Parthenon (unfinished) gapes down
on the black-sailed vessel anchored in the sound.

What I thought was a figure
standing in a doorway
was just a doorway;
the movement in the window
just a loss of light. Look:
my eyes are not my own.

—m—

DEAD CENTRE, 1858

Exactly halfway through his life, panning east
on Princes Street, George Washington Wilson stopped
the moving world into focus. After long exposure,
ghosts returned to their bodies. Calton Hill rose
at the top of the frame, the grave-slots of the cemetery
a perfect *memento*. The first snapshot. Steady traffic.

—···—

ATGET COMES TO EDINBURGH

1. *The Castle*

After the ordered views of Versailles and St. Cloud,
the sign of scissors on every plant and bush,
the Rock scunnered him;
the clutter of stones,
its smoking midden of piled houses:
Paris up-ended on an old volcano,
verminous and cold.

2. *Calton Hill*

He has laboured up the hill before dawn
to see the braided mist in the valley lifting,
the developed city in its liquor of light.
Here are the planned perspectives of man and nature;
formal correspondence; scale and contrast;
a triangular view of history, from a height.
The gardens marking where Renaissance starts.

3. Vertumnus

His hands blackened by chemicals, back
bowed under the weight of the camera,
the holders, plates, tripod, his enormous coat,
he eats the same each day: bread, milk, sugar,
and takes the same position to record the seasons.
They flick past and he speaks the colours:
chlorophyll, honey, cinnamon and *bone*.

—⟋⟋—

EDINBURGH CASTLE (DETAIL)

The Japanese tourist
places his camera on a post,
backs away, and stands,
smiling vigorously.
The small machine flashes; clicks.
I hear the shutter's
granular slither
as a spade in wet soil,
while he would hear: *sha'shin*.

The whirr of winding-on.

He drops the smile,
picks up his Nikon and goes,
muttering about something,
punishing the ground.

—⟋⟋—

'The people were saying no two were e'er wed
But one had a sorrow that never was said,
And I smiled as she passed with her goods and her gear,
And that was the last that I saw of my dear.'

—⁘—

Dearest Chatty—

What an age to be brought into! The journey by steam-train to the Chrystal Palace where I am shewing my Light-Drawings was but twelve hours. Three years past, one was obliged to travel two days (or more) by wooden coach.

But at what cost to our nation? On one hand our Highlands are still being planted with sheep at the expense of People, and those that are not driven to Canada fill our cities. The old ways, and the Gaelic, go with them. On the other, it seems that while our country is diminished, our southern sister grows apace. The price we pay for railways, better roads & speedier mail, is seeing our most able Artists & Scientists leave for London—their places taken by Thomas Cook's travellers, decked in tartan, looking for 'The Picturesque'. It is the end of an old song.

Enough of this. They have bought few of my Pictures, but there is time. A kiss to you & your aunt Mary.

Your loving father

—⁘—

With every step of hers towards the light
a step of mine towards the murk.

—⟪⟫—

My daughter feels no fear
because of me.
I have it learnt
because of her.

—⟪⟫—

SUNNY MEMORIES

The year of the Sheep, the Year of Burning;
we shall return no more; the Rising,
from Glenfinnan to Culloden Moor;
potato famine; Nova Scotia;
Barra, Knoydart, Ardnamurchan.

Balmoral; the Sobieski Stuart Brothers'
Vestiarium Scoticum; clan maps and tartan,
Edinburgh rock; Walter Scott and Harry Lauder;
Wha's like us? Cheers! and *slàinte mhath*
to the king across the water.

—⟪⟫—

THE ROYAL HIGH SCHOOL

After the children had gone
the gulls came, in a white flit:
sentinel at windows,
falling between buildings.

The janitors and cleaners never saw them
dropping in: ambling down corridors,
looking into rooms, blinking
at their new estate.
They nest here now, among the jotters
and pencils, unopened boxes
of *The Scottish Constitution*;
living like kings
on a diet of silverfish,
long-life milk and chalk.

—◌—

They are fading. The damned things are fading. I was to-day shewn some views of the Scott Monument we made in '46—the wretched folly just then finished—and the top is bleached away, with all the edges dimmed. The paper is now going into ugly spots all over, and the image is fast fading out. The light that made it now dismantles it.

Meanwhile from my window the building mocks me in its crisp dressed stone, its hard lines clean against the sky.

How many years wasted? Five? Ten? A life.

May 1856

—◌—

Perhaps they had been hung in sunlight: what little we have here would do it most surely.

Dear Adamson used to speak of the need to wash the Pictures fully, to beware an exhausted fixer. These may be flawed in this respect only.

Or the smoke of the city that gave our light-drawings their filtered subtlety—like an Islay malt, he would say. That must dis-colour & make brittle even the best-made image.

Or the paper and board: that may be the cause.

Or this sea air.

May 1857

—⁂—

I have returned to the Disruption after fifteen years. Today was taken up with greying the hair of ministers.

May 1858

—⁂—

My Dear Chatty—

I write to tell you news you must have long expected—that Amelia and I are to wed. She has been such a strength to me & what work I try to do, and will surely make me finish my Picture. She sees Nature more truly than most that look on Her.

Hence it is a threefold happiness within a year: your marriage to Walter and the joyous news that you will have a child; and now a companion for your ageing father. I am triply blest!

May 1862

—⁂—

I have a grandson, long-limbed & strong, and he will be christened Charley. God save him. Dear Charlotte is much fatigued from her confinement, but joyful.

Let her be a better mother to her son than I was father to her. She will love him as much as I love her, but let her eyes not be taken away by idle foolishness as mine were. All life and hope rest here in the child, in its green of growing.

October 1862

—∽—

My light has gone. Charlotte. I cannot write this. My poor dead child.

The image arrested, the image effaced. All colour bleached out to a sea-blue; all sound to a grief of gulls. I am losing you. Will all my girls turn to ghosts?

I have done <u>nothing</u>: nothing but stand in my own light, my shadow falling on all that lies before me. I am a man beside myself, harm in my heart.

<u>Chatty</u>.

December 1862

—∽—

'Last night she came to me, my dead love came in,
So softly she entered, her feet made no din;
And she put her hand on me, and to me did say,
"It will not be long, love, till our wedding day." '

—∽—

I look in the mirror and see nothing,
then turn to the window
and catch myself walking away.

—⁂—

*I have finished the Disruption painting. It should rest on
Calton Hill with all the other follies of my age: the blind
observatories and the quarter-Parthenon; the monument to
another country's hero; the house of my wasted years.*

*And how many years to make this travesty of Nature?
Twenty-three. And while I laboured, my daughter Charlotte
grew from girl to woman; the Calotypes faded & the min-
isters grew old. I give the world this aberration as token of
my failure. What age was Chatty when she left this life &
took the light from mine? No older. She was twenty-three.*

Newington Lodge, May 1866

—⁂—

AMNESTY IN THE GARDEN

A brim of light leaks out across the sea
to lift the bevel in the wave, the water's lens,
and everything moves again:
the pleated land renewed in its bloom
of gold, the broom and yellow gorse.
Gulls hang their hinges of light
over the loosened water, calling,
calling me down from the hill's height
and the high stones that remain,
what marks we made on them long effaced.

The forest creaks like a door.
Where children will come this morning
to make handsels for the May Queen
—gathering flowers of the forest
to draw the harvest of the sea—
a rabbit scutters in the leaf-litter,
squirrels shrug up trees, and a pheasant
clatters away like a mechanical toy.
Steeped again in the blent green,
A boy enters the walled garden.

A wind. The lilac and laburnum trees
seethe and churn, then settle. Above him,
the buds are swollen and opening;
below, red shoots spirl to the morning sun.
The roots swarm. In the walled garden
form is imposed on this fugitive green,
this rinsing light: to enclose is to make sacred,
to frame life's chaos for a slow repair,
to make an art of healing, of release,
an amnesty against despair.

—⁓—

Night breathes on me
and the world mists.
I make a window
in the mirror
for the face of my father,
tired of this.

—⁓—

I cannot paint. This stroke has done for that. I can write barely, but my mind has clarified. A simple life. I am old, and it is almost over. When people look at me now, they stare, as if through a glass.

Today I was taken by the Water of Leith. The trees in the water. Charley was with us, running ahead, all in green. Eyes closed, the world goes red. A red dress. Lovers move their mouths, their hands. They will go to hidden places to love each other. Opening to green. Everything green. Our great difficulty. Too long looking for light, when green was all that mattered.

If people speak of me, say that I sang a capital song. Slow airs, all of them. For my lost girls. The flowers of the forest. Chatty. It will not be long, love. My last song. Taken from life. A drawing of us all together. Drawing with light, the saddest art: the music of what's gone. Into the turning green.

May 1870

—⁊—

DAVID OCTAVIUS HILL
BORN 1802 DIED 1870
FOR 43 YEARS SECRETARY
TO THE ROYAL SCOTTISH ACADEMY
HE WAS A MAN
OF UPRIGHT NOBLE
AND UNSELFISH CHARACTER
WHO SACRIFICED MUCH
FOR THE ADVANCEMENT OF
THE FINE ARTS OF HIS COUNTRY

THIS MEMORIAL
WAS EXECUTED AND ERECTED BY
HIS SECOND WIFE
AMELIA ROBERTSON PATON

NOTES

'Camera Obscura' is built on the personal and artistic life of David Octavius Hill—an indifferent painter but pioneering photographer in Edinburgh in the mid-19th century. It is mostly concerned with his tragic private life (the death of his second daughter, in infancy, and his wife two years later; the death of Robert Adamson, his creative partner, and the consequent collapse of his photography; the death of Charlotte, his beloved first daughter) and the brief glory, in his middle years, when he made the finest of all early photographs.

In 1843, not long after the death of his wife, Hill witnessed one of the most important events in Scottish history in that century: the Disruption of the Church—where dissident clergy split with the established Church of Scotland. Hill resolved to paint this momentous occasion. In order to conveniently capture the likenesses of the four hundred rebel ministers, Hill's friend Sir David Brewster recommended the new technique invented in England by Fox Talbot—the calotype—and introduced Hill to his subsequent partner and friend, the chemist and photographer Robert Adamson. They set up a studio together at Rock House, Calton Hill, and for four and a half years produced a mass of extraordinary images.

In 1848, Adamson sickened and died. Hill then abandoned photography. Twenty-three years after beginning it, he finished the Disruption Painting; it was an abject failure. When he died in 1870, there was no mention in his obituaries of his groundbreaking work in photography, and his cameras and entire stock were sold for seventy pounds.

Hill's story is also, in a way, the story of Scotland—and, in particular, Edinburgh—during the last flowering of the Enlightenment.

—ɯ—

The imagined diary entries and letters by Hill are counterpointed by a contemporary narrative of the city using views from the *camera obscura* on the High Street by the Castle, and from Calton Hill, where the first *camera* and first observatory were situated.

The remaining poems and fragments—centred on the page—are adjuncts to the main narratives: set out of time and moving between past and present.

—⁂—

p. 60 *The Flowers of the Forest*

A lament for the battle of Flodden, thought to bring bad luck to the piper who plays it, unless he introduces a deliberate error to his delivery.

'*a' wi'ed awae*': Sc. all withered away

p. 60 'My young love said to me'

The first of four verses of the traditional ballad 'She Moved Through the Fair'.

p. 61 *Circus on Calton Hill*

'channer': Sc. grumble
'shedding': Sc. cleaving
'kittling': Sc. becoming excited
'find': Sc. feel with the fingers; indecently handle

p. 62 *Four Views from the Camera Obscura*

'pends': Sc. gateways
'lands': Sc. tenements

p. 78 *Sunny Memories*

The title of a book by Harriet Beecher Stowe, in which she describes the Highland Clearances as 'an almost sublime instance of the benevolent employment of superior wealth and power in shortening the struggles of advancing civilisation'.

p. 78   *The Royal High School*

The proposed seat of the Scottish Parliament had Devolution been won in 1979.

p. 79   'They are fading'

July 1995: the Scott Monument begins to disintegrate during the cleaning process, which is abandoned. Meanwhile, an exhibition of Hill/Adamson calotypes—in perfect condition—opens at the Royal Scottish Academy.

p. 82   *Amnesty in the Garden*

from the Latin *amnestia* and the Greek *amnestos:* oblivion; forgetting; an intentional overlooking.